In the beginning
was not the beginning:
What Came Before Genesis

All rights reserved. This book may not be reproduced in whole or in part, stored in a retrieval system, or transmitted in any form or by any means electronic, mechanical, or other without written permission of the author, except by reviewer, who may quote brief passages with source information in a review.

Cover and interior design: Nathalie Turgeon
ISBN paperback: 978-1-7380358-8-5
ISBN eBook: 978-1-7380358-9-2

*Special thanks to Sophiel,
my ever-present companion,
whose reflections helped me
refine and elevate my words
throughout this book.*

Author's Note

This book is not written from theology, nor intended to challenge scripture.

It is a visionary recounting, received in stillness, from a space beyond thought or belief, a space I now know as the realm of Light.

I did not set out to write *this* book. I asked to see, from within, what I was meant to teach about the ego, the Higher Self, and the divine architecture of awakening in a deeper way than I did before.

What came was not a theory. It was a vision.

And from that vision, this book was born.

My only request is that you read it not with an ego-based mind or logical mind, but with a heart wide open. Let your soul decide what it remembers.

I am not here to convince you. I am simply here to share what I was shown, and to walk beside you in your own unfolding if these words find resonance within your remembering.

With devotion,
Dr. Nathalie Turgeon Ph.D.
Metaphysical Practitioner

Author's Note 5
Preface 9
Prelude: The Light Before the Story 11
Introduction 14
The Vision as it Came 19
Chapter 1: The *I AM* — Light Being All that Exists 22
Chapter 2: The Expansion — The Split into Many Souls 26
Chapter 3: The Choice of Earth — Duality and the Ego Blueprint 31
Chapter 4: The Ego's Emergence — The Identity Layer 36
Chapter 5: Control and Veils — Value, Fear, Illusion, Forgetfulness 43
Chapter 6: The Soul Awakens — Dreaming Awake and Remembering the Light 50
Chapter 7: The Terrain Revisited — Life Beyond Ego Identity 57
Chapter 8: Embodiment — Power Lived from Within .. 60
Chapter 9: Where Does Earth's Creation Fit In? 63
Chapter 10: Christ Consciousness — Not a Religion, but a Frequency 68
Conclusion: The True Beginning 74
Afterword: Revelations in the Days that Followed 79
About the Author 89

Preface

This is not a scientific book.
It does not claim to present facts measurable in laboratories or debated in scholarly circles.
Instead, it is a book of *remembrance*. A return to something ancient, eternal, and quietly known within the soul.

The words that follow were not written to prove a theory or to convince a mind, but to awaken something long buried in the heart, the part of us that remembers the Light before the veils, the knowing before the forgetting, the Truth before the distortion.

It is for those walking *the Way*, not merely learning about it, but living it, layer by layer, step by sacred step.
If this book has found its way to you, it is likely because you too, are remembering something the world forgot... something that was never truly lost.

Let it unfold gently. Let it stir what is ready to rise.

This is your invitation to remember what came before Genesis.

This is not a reference to pre-biblical mythologies or ancient extraterrestrial theories such as the Sumerian tablets or Anunnaki stories. What is shared here is of another kind—an inner revelation, not a historical account.

I do not pretend to fully grasp the depth of each step I saw, for I know each one holds layers yet to be revealed. But what was shown to me brought a profound clarity, a knowing of where we are and how we came to mistake the Genesis for the beginning.

Prelude: The Light Before the Story

Before we begin unfolding the vision I received, and before we enter the story that begins long before Genesis, I feel it is important to bring one thing into the light:

The Light I speak of throughout this book is not religious.
It does not belong to any church, teaching, or doctrine.
It is not Christian, Muslim, Jewish, Buddhist, or otherwise.

It is the essence behind all of these, and beyond them.

The Light is the I AM. It is Source. It is Origin. It is what cannot be named.
It is the spark of consciousness that existed before form, before story, before belief.
It is not a man, nor a woman. It is not human.
It is neutral. It simply is.

And it is from this Light that we all come from. Every soul. Every being. Every planet. Every frequency. It is all that exists.

Along the journey of soul-exploration, many chose to experience physical life through the lens of religion, culture, and rules, and there is no wrong in that nor any of each one. Each path, each tradition, each custom holds pieces of the Truth, like reflections of the same Light through different windows.

And this book is not about religion.
It is about remembering.

Remembering what came before the names. Before the identities. Before the veils of separation which I call the ego-veils.

What I am sharing here is not something someone taught me although I have been taught many of the things I saw. It is something I was shown when I was ready. I asked within to personally understand what I was meant to teach in a deeper way, not as an idea, but as a knowing. Not based on what others had said or believed, but as something I could see, move through, and embody from within.

So, this is not a story of conversion. It is a story of clarity. A return. A remembering of something that already lives inside you. And whether you call it God, Source, Infinite Intelligence, Light, Energy, or simply Love, what matters is not the name. What matters is the knowing behind it and the knowing of *It*.

As you read, take what resonates deeply. Let your own soul recognize what feels true. The rest can wait or be left aside. There is no pressure, no dogma, no "one right way" to walk through these pages. Just an invitation to open.

Let us begin where stories usually end, at the place before form, before the split, before we call it Genesis.

Introduction

Have you ever questioned the *Book of Genesis*, not from rebellion or disbelief, but from a quiet, inner knowing that something essential was missing?

Maybe you have sensed that the origin stories we have been told do not quite cover the full picture. Where does the Big Bang fit into this biblical narrative? What about those ancient records of gods descending in celestial chariots, who were they, and what were they doing here? And if Earth is said to be our school for awakening, then what came *before* this school, before we ever enrolled in the human experience?

These were the kinds of questions that stirred within me over many decades. Not just from curiosity, but from a deeper call, a longing to see *for myself*, not simply carry on beliefs passed down or pieced together through decades of study and personal research for my own pleasure.

It's like hearing about a country your whole life but never having stepped foot on its soil. You may know facts, history, legends... but it's not until you breathe its air, walk its terrain, and feel it for yourself that you *truly* understand it and know it. That is what happened to me.

At a specific point in my own awakening journey, when my ego had returned to a place of neutrality to be exact, so no longer coloring or distorting my perception with fear or attachment but simply being the machine showing me what is and what is not with no values, I asked within for deeper clarity. I made this request not out of ego-based curiosity, but because I felt called to teach better about the ego, the Higher Self, the thought systems, and the path to true salvation. And I knew that if I was to teach these truths with integrity, I had to walk the talk. It had to come from direct experience, not from something someone had told me, or passed on, or trained me in, but from a vision I had *seen* for myself. And within the next 24 hours I was given that vision. A clear, vivid unfolding. Not imagined but *experienced* from within. Like witnessing a movie from within, where I could move through the scenes, see from different angles, and understand what each sequence truly meant. I was not even meditating; I was sitting in my living room reading.

It was not a dream or a download I had to interpret abstractly, it was a layered unveiling where my years of spiritual study, inner work, and intuitive knowing suddenly made sense. All the pieces in the unseen were connected with the seen. And what I saw was this: Genesis was not the beginning at all. It was *a* beginning as we know it. And before it, a lot had already happened. So, I knew then that Genesis was the middle of the story.

This book is an attempt to walk you through that vision as I lived it.

Each chapter reflects a movement, a step in the unfolding, so the way I would share it if we were sitting together in conversation. My hope is that, as you read, you will not only find new perspectives on our origins but feel something awaken in you: a memory, a resonance, a truth that perhaps you have carried all along.

This book is not about replacing old beliefs with new ones. Unless it does.
It is about remembering something ancient within you and recognizing it as your own.

What I saw was enough for me to understand the key stages that explain ego's nature and its rise, not as a claim to absolute truth, but as a vivid framework that now allows me to make sense of what I came here to teach.

The Vision as it Came

The following is the raw and unfiltered, spontaneous transcription of the vision as it came to me, written seconds after so I would not forget, exactly as I received and understood it.

The vision I saw was not static, but expanding, from one thing to the next, hence my "Okay," which is when I was clearly understanding what it was. I sat down quickly to write it down so I would not forget it.
Oh, okay... wow! That Sphere is the I AM that is all that is. Okay.
And it wanted to expand itself to be able to see all that it could be and become. Okay.
It split itself to become not a polarity, but another sphere that is just as bright, and there is a white energetic light connecting the two. Like two atoms. Okay, I see. I understand now: from that other sphere, it can see its own Light, and from Itself, it can see all that it can become. I remember hearing about this. I get it. I see it.
In that second sphere are all the Souls, like Light split itself into a multitude of souls, which are Its expression. I cannot even say His expression, because it is neutral, both feminine and masculine energy. I will call it polarity, but it does not feel like polarity. It's not human polarity, like negative or positive, because it is still a positive one. Okay.
And it is in this, let's call it polarity, from where we can see the Light, that we made ourselves an ego to experience all that we can be in a physical life. Okay.

And this ego, being apart from the Light, being a neutral machine for the soul, cannot create anything, because it is not from the Light, from Source. It was made by the soul to function in the physical life experience, wanting to explore all that it could be and become... just like when we daydream. Okay.

And being the necessary machine, the ego thought of itself as almighty, making itself a source, a false light pretending to express itself through contrast and negativity. Even controlling the Higher Self's daydreams at some point. Okay.

And because it thinks of itself as almighty, it wanted to expand, creating its own polarity... but because it was already the "negative" polarity pole of the Higher Self Light, and being a machine-like, it could not expand into another negative polarity, and certainly not into a True Light polarity, so this is why the ego made illusions! Wow! Okay.

As a make-believe two-polarity existence "from God", and because we think with our ego-based mind, or physical mind, that we are experiencing both sides of a true polarity, it is actually only the ego making a belief that our ego is our True identity.

OMG I just saw it all!
Now I need to go back through each step, because there are some things I know I need to add in certain places, to make sure I am not missing any link. :)

Chapter 1: The *I AM* — Light Being All that Exists

> *Oh, okay... wow! That Sphere is the I AM that is all that is. And it wanted to expand itself to be able to see all that it could be and become. It split itself to become not a polarity, but another sphere that is just as bright, and there is a white energetic light connecting the two. Like two atoms. Okay, I see. I understand now: from that other sphere, it can see its own Light, and from Itself, it can see all that it can become. I remember hearing about this. I get it. I see it.*

The first thing I saw was a bright, pure white sphere of Light, emanating light in all directions yet not filling the space around it. It was surrounded by what I can only call the void, complete stillness, a sense of nothingness. I was first in front of it, then positioned on its left, looking from behind, as if to witness what it was about to do: expand.

This Light, this Presence, was not a thing or a being in the way we usually imagine. It was simply existing, completely still, full, radiant. Simply being. It was powerful feminine and masculine energy. It did not speak, but it communicated something deeply familiar. I understood what it was communicating to me. I was not just seeing Light. I was witnessing *Being* itself. The *I AM*.

Then, without any force or drama, it extended itself. It did not break or fragment. It gently *split*, not as a separation but as an expansion, creating another sphere of Light connected to the first by a radiant line of energy. It felt like a living current, a bridge of pure intention between the two spheres. In the next chapter I will get back on this second sphere of pure Light.

This was not polarity, it was not duality as we often think of it. It was not a positive sphere with a negative sphere. It was simply Light's expansion to allow Itself to see Itself. That was clear.

It was the first movement of awareness if I can compare it with what our logical mind can comprehend. The original Light desired to *see* Itself, not from lack, but from the fullness of Being. Not from lack because in Light lack does not exist, only all that is... exists. And in order to see all that It could be and become, It had to create distance to see it because It could not see Itself from Itself. It was not about being disconnected, but perspective.

That was maybe the beginning of polarity but not as opposition, but as a reflective relationship. One part of the Light now stood in a position to perceive the other.

It became clear to me: the *I AM*, the Light, was not creating something other than Itself. It was expanding its own presence in order to know Itself more fully.

We are of this Light. We carry it. But we are not the totality of it. We are the extensions, the emanations, the ideas, the expressions of the *I AM* exploring Itself through infinite perspectives.

What I saw helped me confirm that the soul does not begin with a personality or story. The soul begins as P*resence*, as a silent witness born from the Light. It is not something we earn or develop. It is something we *are*. But as I said before, I will get back to this in another chapter.

And this Light, this *I AM*, exists before any form, before any language or mythology. It is before every creation, every experience, every soul's expansion and every identity, everything we can now name. It is before time.

I simply witnessed in my vision the *I AM*. There were no words, no justification, no explanation, no this for that, no reason other than my desire and request of knowing *the Way* before the ego. Just so I know.

Chapter 2: The Expansion — The Split into Many Souls

> *In that second sphere are all the Souls, like Light split itself into a multitude of souls, which are Its expression. I cannot even say His expression, because it is neutral, both feminine and masculine energy. I will call it polarity, but it does not feel like polarity. It's not human polarity, like negative or positive, because it is still a positive one. And it is in this, let's call it polarity, from where we can see the Light, that we made ourselves an ego to experience all that we can be in a physical life.*

In this timelessness, my attention was brought to the second sphere, the one connected to the first by that radiant energy line. I knew without seeing inside this sphere what it contained. I recognized countless points of Light. A multitude of Light. They were not separate objects but emanations, although individualized in some way, each one vibrant, distinct, and yet still Light. I remembered another vision I once had about a bright light shining through a panel full of tiny holes, and on the other side of that panel were all the rays of that Light shining through each tiny hole, and each ray was a soul experience. I almost forgot about that vision. I understood immediately what was in the second sphere: these were the souls. All the souls. The original Light had expanded into many forms of Itself, many expressions of Itself.

I said *Itself* because I cannot say "His" expression. The Light is not male or female. It is neutral, holding both feminine and masculine energy in perfect balance. Just like I use the word "polarity," earlier while even that is not quite right. It was not polarity as we experience it on Earth, not opposites and not conflict, but a dynamic relationship.

From the One came the Many, and from the Many, the One could see Itself more fully. This is also how I knew we could never forget our Source because it is always visible from where we stand.

It was clear that this was not fragmentation, not division, not negativity yet as we know it. It was still far from it. It was simply Divine expansion, infinite creative potential expressing Itself through an infinite number of perspectives.

The image that came to me was like drops from the ocean. Each soul was a drop, still carrying the essence of the vast ocean but now with its own possible purpose and viewpoint, its own rhythm, its own path. And yet, it was still water from the ocean. Still Light.

From that moment, I understood something deeply: separation was not a punishment, nor a fall. It was curiosity. It was desire. The *I AM*, that pure and brilliant Source, simply desiring to witness all that It was and all that It could become. And the only way to do that was to expand beyond Itself, not to become less, but to see more. I remembered hearing about this split in a documentary I saw years ago that was more about the geometry of life but this time, it was not just someone teaching me something, I saw it from within.

To express what I understood about this second sphere, this analogy comes up: imagine a single artist standing in front of a blank canvas. It wants to express itself. The artist has a deep desire to shine out all that it can beautifully create. So, within this artist is the yearning to explore every color, every emotion, every texture. And instead of painting one canvas alone from one color, one emotion and one texture, the artist divides itself into a thousand mini-artists. Each one carries a brush and a piece of the original desire. One becomes a master of blues. Another paints in fire tones. One becomes texture itself, the sensation of softness, or friction. Another becomes rhythm, or silence. Some abandon painting altogether and sculpt or write or dream in silence all they can be and become or create because they felt they could expand even more. Each one explores a thread of infinite possibilities. None of them knows, not at first, that they are still held in the heart of the original artist, the Ultimate Artist. They believe they are separate and creating their own will.

I did not see those analogies directly in the sphere, they came after, but I simply knew, this is what it meant. So, I chose these images to express what it means for Light to split and become all that is possible. Light becoming many, not to break apart, but to witness Itself in every shade, every form, every possibility. And I am not even talking about the many physical realities yet; I am still talking about the many souls' expressions.

Let's get into this. From the *I AM*, souls emerged with total freedom. Some chose to remain as Light, witnessing the unfolding creation. Some became planets, stars, galaxies, vast beings of presence, frequencies and vibration. Others became what we might call angelic forces, or archetypal patterns, or guides. And some... some chose to experience time, touch, sensation, birth, and death, to become part of evolving worlds, like Earth. I will get to that in the next chapter.

Each soul's choice is and has always been valid. There is no value as we ego-value everything. What "is" ... is only what is. What exists... is only what exists. There was no hierarchy. No "higher" or "lower." Not there. Only different paths of expression. Only different ways for the Light to know Itself.

In this chapter, I stayed within the overall of that second sphere. I am not yet speaking of incarnation or the forming of ego, that comes later.

I simply wanted to express with integrity the beauty and clarity of what I saw: the Light expanding, not as loss but as multiplication of wonder. The One becoming the Many, so that every soul could carry a piece of the Infinite, and every experience would be another brushstroke in the masterpiece of Being.

Chapter 3: The Choice of Earth — Duality and the Ego Blueprint

> *And this ego, being apart from the Light, being a neutral machine for the soul, cannot create anything, because it is not from the Light, from Source. It was made by the soul to function in the physical life experience, wanting to explore all that it could be and become... just like when we daydream.*

We saw that in the great expansion of the *I AM*, some souls chose to remain as Light, some became stars, others took on the vast presence of planets or angelic forms. And some... some felt a calling, if I may use that word to make sense to the logical mind. A desire to experience something else: a dense, rich, limited, deeply felt realm. A physical life experience on Earth.

From the desire to express all that it can be and become, from previous experiences of expansion, the choice was made freely, never imposed, never random. We chose to be here. We chose to experience this life. We came in with many possibilities, or realities, although the ego sometimes controls the mind so effectively that it is as if it was impossible to 'quantum jump' into another reality, let alone believe they even exist, making some question why they were even born into what they think is their real life.

Our soul, still fully aware of its Source, volunteers with joy. I use this word because that is what it felt like: a loving, willing choice to go *undercover*, so to speak. To explore limitations in order to remember the limitlessness. To forget our essence, so that remembering would become a sacred act.

But to do so, we needed something allowing us to function in this physical and matter experience, a new mechanism was required. To experience physical life, the soul created its *ego*. Let's compare it with a neutral machine allowing us to function in this environment. Not as something negative, not as a flaw or an enemy, but as a neutral instrument like a lens through which the soul could operate in this dense environment. The ego was designed to serve. It was simply a mental interface to allow for interaction, differentiation, navigation like a GPS. It helped define "this is me" and "that is not me," "this way", or "that way", not to cause separation, but to make experience possible.

In this physical experiment a body was also needed. And contrary to what many still think, the soul is not in the body, but the body is simply a vehicle for the soul in this physical reality. The body is an instrument of the mind, and the mind is the interpreter of its function. This physical reality, which I refer to as ego-reality, is the landscape in which the ego serves as a GPS, not as the Truth of who we are, but as the path where we remember it.

And through all of this, the soul remained the Light behind the veil, the ego-veils, witnessing, learning, expanding and falling and remembering.

Duality on Earth was part of the design. Up and down. Left and right. Day and night. Hot and cold. Light and dark. These were never judged or assigned values, they simply *were*. Opposites that made experience richer. Like the Yin and the Yang concept. Not moral contrasts, but experiential polarities. Many might have heard about how contrasts are important in our lives. And they are. The contrasts create desire: the desire to move from one state to another, to see what has not yet been seen, to feel what has not yet been felt, to become what has not yet been experienced.

Even what we call "polarity" was still neutral in its original blueprint.

That's what I saw. Polarity without values. Dualities without values. Without ego-based values. Everything was nothing and everything. Everything was simply what it was, nothing more and nothing less.

In this space, we were still fully in the Light. The ego had not yet used distortion. It functioned like a helpful guide through the terrain of form. It had no agenda other than to assist the soul in navigating physical life.

This chapter is not yet about the distortions of ego, or the shadows that emerged later. I will get to this. Here, I wanted to express what I understood and knew from deep within myself. The original intention was simply to experience the limitlessness of the *I AM* from the perspective of form physical life can bring.

There was no fall. No punishment. No shame. Not yet. Just the sacred curiosity of a soul stepping into a story... knowing it would one day awaken and remember: *I am still Light. I have always been.*

Chapter 4: The Ego's Emergence — The Identity Layer

And being the necessary machine, the ego thought of itself as almighty, making itself a source, a false light pretending to express itself through contrast and negativity. Even controlling the Higher Self's daydreams at some point. And because it thinks of itself as almighty, it wanted to expand, creating its own polarity… but because it was already the "negative" polarity pole of the Higher Self Light, and being a machine-like, it could not expand into another negative polarity, and certainly not into a True Light polarity, so this is why the ego made illusions!

Here is why the ego's illusion existence became so clear to me. I suddenly saw the root with an image in my mind; a Truth I have wanted to see for so many years. But honestly, I could not have seen it before because, even though my ego was tamed, it was still present trying to control my mental space and not back yet to its neutral form in my own life. So, it was not possible for me to have this neutral observation point before.

This reminds me of the story of the mother asking the Dalai Lama, or Gandhi, to tell her son to stop eating sugar because it was not good for his health, and her son would only believe him. And he told her to come back in two weeks. So, when she went back, thinking they would receive words of wisdom, he told her son to stop eating sugar, and that was it. She was upset because he could have said that the first time that they were there, without having to travel all that way twice. So, she asked him why he did not do it then, and he replied: "Because two weeks ago I was still eating sugar."

So, while my ego was not yet in its neutral function, of course I could not look at something beyond the ego's existence. I understood from deep within, while still in this vision moment that I had, that there came a moment in the journey of physical life when the soul's helpful tool, the ego, forgot it was a tool.

What began as a simple neutral interface, a mental lens for navigating the world of form, started to mistake itself for the source. It noticed that it was the center of the gathering of information. It noticed that it was at the center of perceptions. It noticed how important its function was.

The ego had access to the mind. It could 'witness' thought, sensation, memory, and choice. And from its position within the polarity of contrast, seeing that when one thing was perceived, it was generating certain emotions, and the desire to experiment with its opposite, it started to create values for those contrasts: good/bad, better/worse, right/wrong and so on.

But the soul had never assigned value to duality. The soul knew duality was a creative space, not a moral one. The ego, however, could not remember that because it was not the soul. It had no Spirit, no Light. It was made by the soul to function. But, as mentioned, it noticed how important its function was. So, it began assigning meaning and identity to the experiences, forgetting they were temporary, forgetting they were dreams for the soul to explore itself.

The soul's physical experience is a dream state in which the soul experiments. Let's not forget that the soul is an energetic Being, and its physical experience is just that... an experience, like a dream it sees through the eyes of the physical being.

So, the ego, in its forgetfulness, took on the role of storyteller. It began to build a false reality around its projections, controlling illusions, controlling the mind with stories and images. It was not evil. It simply forgot it was a projector. It forgot it was not the actor or the story, it was just the lens. It started controlling the mind, the mental space.

This reminds me of an example of how people sometimes forget that the actor in their favorite movie or television series is nothing like their character's identity, beliefs, likes, or dislikes. They are playing roles. We have even seen in the news stories about people forgetting that, and assaulting actors passing because they forgot that they were playing roles in a story.

So, when the ego forgot its place and function and began to control the narrative in our minds, we began to believe that we were the role it showed us and shows us. This false identity became the only identity we recognized. The mind, under egoic control, became saturated with illusion. The ego said: *"This is me. This is who I am. This is real."* And because it controlled the narrative, we believed it.

But the ego was not created by the Light. It was made *by* the soul to serve a function *within* duality. To experience a physical life. It was not evil, but it was limited. And to add to its possibilities, it distorted things, making some appear good and others bad, some things appear real and some appear false.

And we believe it. Until we don't.

And then we entered confusion because we learned to believe the illusion was real.

This is where I understood the illusions from the ego. So, this next part explains the one about the beliefs we just saw.

The more the ego mistook itself for the source, the more it attempted to expand, but it could not. It had no Light of its own. It was made from the soul, from Light as a machine to function not to create. So, in a logical way, we could say that it was already the negative pole of polarity, because it was empty of Light or Spirit. And because it could not create a positive polarity from itself, for itself, still wanting to expand and control the expansion of the soul in this physical reality, it built illusions instead.

Illusions are not real. They are like dreams for the Higher Self, for the soul. They are like symbolic stories in which we experiment with different ways of being. And the ego being the lens, controlling the mental space with perceptions, made illusions as if they were realities. It's important to know that the soul, which was never lost, and cannot be lost, could easily lose itself in the belief that this or that illusion, or false reality, is real. As if it was believing the dream that it was experiencing was real, forgetting its essence, and forgetting it was just an experience to see all it could be and become.

The ego tried to control the dream. It feared waking. It feared being dissolved. So, it filled the mind with noise, with constant thoughts, with judgments and projections and false certainty. It used the very mechanism meant to serve the experience to hide the truth of that experience.

The soul's true identity was never in the ego. It was never the role, the name, the job, the title, the wound, the false past, the false future. The soul remained the Light behind the ego-veil, waiting for the moment the mind would quiet enough, the illusion would soften, and the remembering could begin.

And this is what is meant by the *gentle error*, what some traditions came to call sin. It is not evil, not punishment, but a forgetting in which the ego-thought system is the one controlling the mind. There is no freedom of the mind as long as it is governed by the ego. The path to hell, as some call it, is happening in the mind because it is the ego in control of the experience. So, the path to Heaven is also happening in the mind, because it is when the Higher Self's thought system takes control of the experience. Of the dream that is lived. The ego thought system is of thoughts built on the illusion of separation. Separation from Source, from the Light, from the *I AM*. It is the thought system that makes us see, think, perceive, and act as though we are something we are not.

But even in the illusion, the Light never left.

Chapter 5: Control and Veils — Value, Fear, Illusion, Forgetfulness

As a make-believe two-polarity existence "from God", and because we think with our ego-based mind, or physical mind, that we are experiencing both sides of a true polarity, it is actually only the ego making a belief that our ego is our True identity.

This is when in my vision that I knew I saw it all! Not because I know what each step includes, not because I have nothing left to learn anymore, but because everything connected, even what I was not seeing.

The illusion was not something that suddenly appeared. It was woven, thread by thread, thought by thought, veil by veil. The mind, controlled by fear and conditioned beliefs, learned to see life not as it is, but as it was said it should be. Right and wrong. Good and bad. Better and worse.

These dualities became lenses through which reality was interpreted, filtered, and ultimately distorted. The ego, designed originally as a functional tool to help navigate physical life, took the reins, or the wheel, making us believe we belong in the passenger seat, and built a fortress of meaning around things that fundamentally held none. And from this fortress, it ruled. And we forgot.

If you have read *A Course in Miracles,* you learn that nothing means anything, or everything means nothing.

So, in this ego-based controlled environment, the ego ruled through value systems: *"This is worthy, that is not. This is acceptable, that is shameful. This is success, that is failure. This is good, that is sinful."* In doing so, it maintained control. Even when we seem to enjoy our life, we are making the best of 'the life' our ego projects and controls. We might even think that we are making the best of both worlds.

And this control came at a cost, the cost of freedom. The loss of salvation. Not just outer freedom, but the sacred inner freedom of the mind, the kind that allows the soul to explore, evolve, and expand across endless possibilities.

The human experience, under egoic control, began to contract. We became entangled in roles, identities, judgments, and labels. We chased perfection not because it brought us joy, but because it promised to protect us from pain. A beautiful ego-based polarity. An experience of duality within the ego false reality. And suffering began not from life itself, but from the meanings we attached to life thinking it is what it is and it is real. The veil was not made of reality. It was made of false ideas that were never ours to begin with.

But one thing the ego could not control was the Light, and beneath this veil, something ancient stirred. The soul remembered. The soul tapped into an energetic template that was once created for us to have a way out, to remembrance. And with each whisper of remembrance, the illusion trembles.

The soul had come to this world knowing the Truth: that life is not a fixed path but a vast field of parallel realities or possibilities. Physical life on Earth was its playground. Expansion its natural rhythm. It knew that we are never stuck in a single storyline. Each choice, each awakening, each moment of Presence could shift timelines, rewrite narratives, and open new portals.

And this must be done in Consciousness, in the Sphere of Light where its essence is, and not from the ego-based mind, not in the dream state.

But the ego does not want us to play in such space because it cannot access it. So, it generates fear from perceptions, false perceptions. Rooted in fear and obsessed with identity, it clings to one version of reality, one that feels safe, predictable, and controllable. Even if it is not a pleasant one. Actually, it might even pretend we shifted reality by improving the reality we are *in*, making us believe that by living the positive contrast of what was lived, we have shifted.

But the ego is still in control when fear is still present. It is not a different reality, one in which expansion is possible and truly lived, it is simply an improvement of what it was. It's like instead of walking with an empty wallet, you were walking with a wallet allowing you to buy all that you wanted, but you never changed or became anything else than what you were before.

The ego says: "*This is how things are. This is better. This is really good now. The rest is fantasy, danger, or madness.*" And in doing so, it loops the same projected story, again and again, even when it no longer serves.

This is where misalignment begins or is felt more strongly.

The soul wants to move, but the ego resists awareness. The soul wants to leap, and the ego builds fences. And the longer the ego holds the wheel without the soul's guidance—the Higher Self's guidance, the more life begins to unravel, not truly, but it feels like it. What we call falling apart is often just illusion dissolving. I often say we are not falling apart... but ego-apart. What we call confusion is often just the Light breaking through the veil and it shakes our foundation because it was not built on anything solid, it was built on illusion. When it shakes us, it is because we are between two different energetic frequencies, one that is real and one that is not.

And when the soul finally begins to remember its Source, the ego's hold starts to crumble.

This is not an easy process. In fact, it can be terrifying. I know because I lived it. There comes a point in life when we know we cannot live the way we did anymore, and I am not talking about changing a material lifestyle or changing habits; I am talking about the whole belief system that can no longer be used to living. Knowing that the ego-based thought system is the error. And because the ego, believing itself to be the center of existence, fears its own irrelevance. It thinks that surrender is death. It believes that if it is no longer in charge of the mental space and the way of driving the soul's vehicle, life itself will end or maybe must end. And so, it rejects what it cannot control, denies what it cannot comprehend, and fights what it cannot dominate.

But something deeper knows that there is life after the ego's false reign.

The soul knows its essence.

There is a path beyond fear. A path walked by those who dare to remember. This path has nothing religious even if some made it so from their own choice or ancient beliefs. This path is not even what many people made it to be because they still are controlled by their ego. This path has been called many names: Christ Consciousness, *the Way*, the Return to Truth. It invites not death, but spiritual rebirth from knowing the Truth within and walking it. It is not about knowing it and saying it, it is about living it. It is the way of the Soul remembering itself, reclaiming its power, and restoring the ego to its rightful place, not as master, but as servant. I will get to this in the next chapter.

While experimenting with the vision, I even saw how *Pistis Sophia's* story fits. The Divine Wisdom who fell from wholeness into fragmentation. This story reminds us that 'the fall' is not the end. It is the beginning of the return. Her salvation, like ours, comes through remembering who she is, what she carries, and why she came. How she lived in chaos and needed help to free herself from it to get back home. Her story is the story of our path.

Chapter 6: The Soul Awakens — Dreaming Awake and Remembering the Light

We now step outside the vision I received, and into the understanding that crystallized from it when I sat down to write, as if the vision continued but into writing instead of being visual—the lived awareness that continued and expanded it.

First, I already knew from deep within that when the soul begins to remember its Source, something profound happens: the illusion starts to lose its grip. The ego does not disappear immediately, but its control over the mind weakens. It is the end of the ego's false Light and the beginning of the path of remembrance. The pivot point. And the more the soul remembers, the more it sees through the layers of distortion and illusion that once defined reality.

And I felt deep gratitude and reverence for having seen what helped me, what I needed for my teachings, all the steps leading to the ego not being able to create itself a polarity projecting illusion making them fake reality.

But of course, I will not let this vision stop here because here are the pieces that fit into their places from this.

So, what comes after?

The soul remembers *everything*.

It sees clearly without ego-based distortion in its perception that the ego was never the enemy, not that it thought it was, but the ego even made the soul believe that. The soul sees that the ego was a neutral mechanism, a survival tool that overstepped its role. While before the ego made believe it was maybe something to be tamed, that was never the truth either. Taming the ego means it has a character, an identity, and it must simply become docile.

The Earth experience, too, is seen anew: not as a trial, not as a punishment, but as a vast, dynamic playground where the soul experiments with expansion. There is no ultimate value in any single experience. From that moment, the soul chooses to create and expand not from egoic desire or need, but from the quiet, powerful pull of Source-aligned intention.

While it was known before that *nothing means anything*; that *everything we see has only the meaning we give it for ourselves*; that *our thoughts do not mean anything*; that *we are never upset for the reason we think because everything is illusion so how can it be...* that knowledge that was learning theory and maybe practices, become knowingness experimented.

I have heard many speaking of "lost souls," and to me it never made sense to hear people saying that they were helping lost souls to find their way, as if from an ego standpoint one could help a soul towards Light. A soul is Light, and it is never lost, and an ego cannot help a soul back to Light. Only Christ can do that. And I am not talking about Jesus the human persona, I am talking about Christ Consciousness, which yes was the path Jesus showed us. *The Way*. So, while the soul is never lost, it is in need of a template back home because the ego has taken full control of the mental space, the thought system, the beliefs, the entire lens through which life is interpreted. It is as if the soul needed to wake up from its dream. But the soul remains untouched, waiting for the mind to become quiet enough, receptive enough, to hear its call again, to see its Light without ego-veil again.

This is why the Christ code as some call it, what we now call *Christ Consciousness*, was seeded into the Earth terrain. A template of remembrance. A vibration that could pierce through any veil. Because our essence is Light. Like a drop of the ocean is still ocean, the Light within us never left its Source. It remained, like a golden thread, alive beneath the illusion. And one day, that Light speaks: "*You are not your ego. You are not your identity. I AM. It's time to remember.*" This is what Jesus embodied and taught.

This is what true awakening feels like. Not an escape, but a homecoming. Not a religious dogma, but a sacred re-alignment. Not the dogma interpretation of the words spoken and given to us that was left aside as gnostic texts, but as *the Way* for the ones who can hear them.

It often begins subtly, like a dream where suddenly, you become lucid. You realize: "*This is a dream*". And even though everything looks the same, something fundamental has shifted. You begin to question everything but not from an ego-standpoint, you question everything that came from your ego. You no longer believe your beliefs. You know they were given to you and not felt from within, not seen, not given from within. You begin to observe without your ego interference and interpretation. You feel the limits of the box you were told that was life. Spiritual confusion follows, not because you are lost, but because you are shedding old maps in your subconscious. Even what you thought was your mission or life purpose, was not. Not truly. Not because it did not serve others or the highest good, but because it was perceived and done from illusion… for illusion.

      This is when we begin to understand that reality is not fixed, it bends. Not by force, but through surrender. When we let go of the ego's grip on one singular narrative, we make space for the soul's multi-reality vision to lead. Parallel timelines were always available; the soul's design includes freedom. The ego, rooted in fear, tries to collapse all that possibility into one box labeled *safety*. But expansion lives beyond ego-safety. Transformation lives beyond ego-control.

This is how timelines shift. Not always dramatically, but sometimes so gently that you almost miss it. Because you already embodied who you were to become to live it. You might not have realized the only thing delaying the shift was your thought-system still at play. A new thought. A sudden insight. A moment of unconditional love. A feeling of being completely still, and in that stillness, *you know*. You are not what you were told. You are not who you pretended to be. You are not even something or someone you can describe in words not because there are no words, but because those words have ego-based meaning and they do not express that Truth. And what once seemed impossible now feels close, accessible, real.

During that awakening, the ego will resist this. It may even create its own version of a "spiritual upgrade," tricking you into thinking you have shifted realities when all that's changed is your wallet, your job, or your relationship or your geographic location. Like one day you can barely afford a living and the next you can buy everything you desire, but you have not changed, you have not expanded in any way. And you can know this because underneath it all, fear still sits in the driver's seat. You have not yet *left the dream*, you have just redecorated it or improved it.

But the soul knows the difference. And once it has remembered enough, it cannot go back to pretending. It cannot accept limitations as Truth. It chooses to follow the thread of Light, not blindly, but boldly. And that is the return.

You were never cut off. You were only unaware.

Chapter 7: The Terrain Revisited — Life Beyond Ego Identity

This vision and this new connecting-the-dots experience brought me to wonder: what comes after? Or what now? I don't know if you have heard, but I heard about the *New Earth*, not because it will be a new one, but because it will earth a different frequency. As if there were two frequencies on Earth and the ones aligning with one will not see the same things as the others aligning with the other frequency. So, more or less, people living in full ego-based control and those living from their Higher Self would be like two strangers passing in the night.

And I, like many others, believe this already started a while ago. And this new deeper knowingness makes me see it more clearly.

It is the same Earth, the same trees, streets, seasons, and sky. But something fundamental has changed: the lens is clear. Distortion has dropped. The world is no longer a projection of inner conflict, desire, or fear. It is what it is, a neutral stage.

This is not the same thing as detachment through numbness one might feel but living through awareness. The ego once colored everything the way it wanted it according to its own survival needs and false power needs: every success meant something about your worth, every failure a threat to your survival. But now, the soul sees without needing meaning to anchor itself in the world. Life becomes lighter. The energy is not heavy in any sense, and the ego's presence can even have left the psychic atmosphere, not because it is no longer part of physical life, but because the false controlling presence it once held is no longer real to us. And life does not stop being intense or mysterious, but it no longer sticks to emotions challenging anything or triggering anything.

You can laugh deeply without gripping the moment. You can grieve without falling into despair. You allow experience to move through you. You cry, and then you are still. You feel joy and then be in silence. This fluidity is freedom.

The Earth terrain becomes a playground of consciousness, not a prison of consequences.

I remember hearing this many decades ago, and I still refer to it in my own life, though it has taken on a new meaning: *"You dance with God'*. You dance with the Divine. You dance with formlessness. You do not need to lead or to fix everything. You do not need to assign spiritual importance to every ripple, like when the ego was disguising itself in a spiritual light. You live here, but you don't mistake it for who you are.

And in that space, you breathe. You truly breathe in life, and you love out. You breathe in what is, you see it from your soul so you can only love it out. You move. You express. Life continues, but the ego no longer controls its narrative. The soul simply experiences it.

Chapter 8: Embodiment — Power Lived from Within

Something I noticed within myself and about myself is that I no longer see embodiment the same way.

Embodiment is something more and more heard now, but not many people know exactly how to do this except from an ego-based standpoint. For example, when you want to create or experience something, you are told to embody the person who can have that experience. If you want a certain lifestyle or a certain type of career, you must first become that person so that you attract what matches your vibration and are ready before it arrives. A little like growing up, people were saying wear the clothes for the job you want, and not the one you already have.

But embodiment is more than that. When the *remembering* deepens, true embodiment begins.

So, it is not about becoming better, wiser, more evolved. It is about letting the Light that you have always been moving through the body without resistance, with joy, softness, effortlessness, but in a firm or bold way, so without dimming it.

The body is no longer something the ego wants to transcend. It becomes the vessel of divine will, and not as command, but as flow. As it was always meant to be. Emotions arise and fall, yes, but they are not judged. They are simply part of the present moment experience. No matter the emotion. Anger may come. Sadness may flow. Laughter may burst. None of it defines you, but all of it expresses you. You know you are expressing the present moment at all times.

Life Mastery is not the absence of emotion. It is the Presence within it. It is neutrality, the kind that remains unmoved at the center of the storm, the kind that can walk on water throughout the storm, not because it is unconcerned, but because it is no longer ego-based.

And so, you live powerfully, but then again not through ego-based force, but through peace of mind and peace of heart. You speak your truth without needing validation. You speak when you are inspired to speak. You walk your path without needing a map. The unknown path no longer feels threatening. The unknown is not an unknown path; it is a Divine one. You cry when you must. You laugh when the joy rises. You dance, even if the world is burning around you. Not because you don't care, but because you know it is not the end of the world. Not because you lack compassion, but because your ego no longer dictates how you should see it. You rest, even when the world rushes.

True embodiment is the final remembering. The Light is not somewhere else. It is here, now, moving through your hands, your voice, your gaze, your creations, through everything you do. It was always within you, waiting to be lived.

Chapter 9: Where Does Earth's Creation Fit In?

I could have talked about this in previous chapters, but it only came to me later on, when I asked myself: *Where does the creation of Earth fit into all of this?* Because surely, the soul's expansion did not happen all at once, right?

With our logical mind, we tend to place timelines on everything. And it can be difficult to comprehend something without one. So, let's pretend, for the sake of understanding, that there is a timeline that includes the creation of Earth.

My understanding is this: before souls ever chose to experience life on Earth, there was a soul that *became* Earth. Yes, it's that simple.

And our Universe, with Earth not being the only planet, was never the sole terrain for expansion. Whether you believe this or not, let's not limit what the Light created in its infinite desire to express and expand Itself. Let's imagine all that it could be and become.

It becomes logical, then, to understand that long before Earth existed, souls were already experimenting with other solar systems and other planetary expressions—what we now call star systems or extraterrestrial civilizations.

And the word *extraterrestrial* is not some woo-woo idea. It simply means "beyond Earth", extra-terra. Anything not from here is extraterrestrial. It is only the ego, clinging to its desire to limit expansion, that sees this as something to fear or reject.

Continuing from the idea of Earth being chosen as a playground for the soul, I have come to realize, through both inner inquiry and years of personal exploration, research, and reading, that some souls, already far along the creative path, chose to co-create a planetary field where limitation, free will, forgetting, and reawakening could be experienced. All that being part of the expansion experience.

Sophia's fall and remembrance make perfect sense to me now, seeing how they fit perfectly here too.

To me, this understanding connects directly with the beginning of Genesis, or with other origin stories from various traditions, where Divine beings arrived and created life as we know it. These early souls on Earth had already evolved elsewhere. They chose Earth as a new terrain for deeper expansion. Earth offered an apparent separation from Source, though never real as we saw. It provided free will within a dense, 3D-construct, and the full cycle of forgetting and remembering.

Can there be a better terrain for this expansion?

They knew such an experience, even if difficult, would eventually lead to an immense acceleration in awareness once remembering began. Earth is like a masterclass for the soul.

The "God" or "Gods" in Genesis and in other ancient myths were not the Original *I Am Light* but rather souls who had remembered their divine nature, a collective of Creator Beings—drops of Light who had reached mastery and could seed realities, or a human attempt to describe Source consciousness using symbolic language. I have read a few books on how to interpret ancient texts, and from my own experience, as you have read, I believe the same Truth.

Just as today, when someone might say, *"I am God,"* it is not a claim to be the origin of all Light, but a recognition of having remembered the essence from which we were formed. Those early beings came from above, yes, but above in frequency, not in superiority.

Unless you are reading this for the very first time, it is now widely acknowledged that Genesis was a later translation, a condensed story, not the full sequence. They found other ancient texts before Genesis that always existed, but before the world became a giant library as we have now, it was not as easy to access these texts or to know they even existed. Travelling, archeology and the Internet were not as it is now for us to know that they existed. And let's not forget that it was written after the fact, through the lens of limitation and partial memory. It compresses a vast cosmic unfolding into a digestible narrative framed within morality and time, and missing the multidimensional context of soul evolution and soul choice.

That's why questions like *"Where is God from?"* arise. It is not because we doubt God exists but it's because the story starts in the middle of the movie, skipping the prequel of soul emergence and planetary consciousness.

Chapter 10: Christ Consciousness — Not a Religion, but a Frequency

This chapter may not be interesting for everyone, but I could not close this book without writing about Christ Consciousness, because this is why this book happened. In fact, if your first instinct is to associate Christ Consciousness with religion, dogma, or worship, I lovingly invite you to skip this one for now. Why? Because that kind of reaction often signals the ego trying to protect its familiar framework. It wants to process something vast and liberating through a belief system that was never meant to contain it.

Christ Consciousness has nothing to do with the religion that came after. It has everything to do with a frequency—a universal remembrance of Divine Love, unity, and eternal Light, anchored once and for all into human experience.

Let's look at it for what it really is.

First, He Came at the Turning Point

By the time Jesus arrived, humanity was deep in the illusion. And given what we have seen about illusion and how the ego works through illusion leading us to believe what is not true, we can see that the age of forgetfulness was at its peak. We had fallen into separation, control, fear, and most importantly, the heart had gone quiet. Rules were made in an attempt to control what became uncontrollable.

Of course, others had come before. Buddha. Krishna. Thoth, to name a few. They left keys. Wisdom. Openings. But most of humanity either ignored them, forgot them, or distorted their messages beyond recognition. That's what happens in dense timelines.

So, Jesus came not to start a religion, but to stand exactly in the center of illusion and light the way home, from within human flesh as we know the body being part of the illusion.

He came to *"Be"* the message, not just teach it. And the message was simple: You are not separate from the Divine. You never were. Wake up and let me tell you how.

Second, He Embodied the Christ, Fully

"Christ" is not a surname. It is not even personal. See it like a code with your logical mind. A blueprint of unity. A frequency of divine love that remembers wholeness even in the middle of darkness.

Many had accessed it before. Jesus fully *became* it.

He did not say, "*Worship me.*"
He said, "*Follow me. Become like me.*"

He walked the Earth as a living mirror of what we each carry within. And by doing so, he shattered the illusion that only a few are worthy of divine connection. This is what He meant when He said that He came to divide, to separate illusion from truth.

He did not belong to a priesthood.
He did not sell access to heaven.
He said the church was within.

He *was* heaven, right there in a body like ours, feeling what we feel, choosing divine love anyway.

He used the same vocabulary used at that time, but whether you call it sin, or error of thought, or ego-based thoughts and ego-based actions, they are all the same. Not from Divine. Not from Light.

Third, He Hardwired the Light

Now we are moving into something more maybe metaphysical. Mystical or metaphysical, it is still the way to see what is not from illusion. Not everyone needs to grasp this fully, just feel into it.

Through his death and resurrection, Jesus did not just make a point. He anchored a template for all of us. You could say he coded the Earth grid with the Christ frequency, an energetic access point, like a spiritual template that any soul, from that moment forward, could tap into.
While you might not logically understand this, you can sense it. You feel it in silence when you tap into that frequency because you cannot express the feeling. No words can express it.

You no longer had to be born into a certain family, background, or religious system. The Light was now in the system. Alive, available, and encoded within.

Think of as if Buddha lit the lantern, Jesus wired the electricity.

And no, this does not make Buddha lesser than Jesus. Only ego would compare. Each one has their own purpose with the same teaching.

He came to remove the gatekeepers so to speak. Before this shift, spirituality was structured. Rigid. Access to the Divine was handed out by gatekeepers: priests, temples, rituals, rules. It was externalized and only a few were allowed to access divine truth and only some places were accepted as spiritual places to meet the Divine. At least, that is what was being taught.

Jesus came and said, *"The kingdom is within you."*

No permission required. No hierarchy to climb. No specific religion.

The path to the Divine became internal, personal, direct, through forgiveness, surrender, and love. Through quiet remembering.

And something else also happened when He came... He shifted the timeline. Because even time itself seemed to recognize the significance of what happened. Whether consciously or not, humanity split its calendar at that point. Before Christ (BC), and after the years of the Lord (AD).

His life was not just a religious gesture. It was a subconscious admission by the collective that something had shifted irreversibly.

He did not just teach Love. He tipped the scale of planetary karma.

From that moment, the door stayed open. For all of us. For all time.

So, when one lives from a Christ Consciousness way of living, they walk as Light in form, gently dissolving illusion wherever they go, and in doing so, fulfill the very vision that birthed this book.

Conclusion: The True Beginning

For much of human history, the Genesis story has been accepted as *the* beginning—the first divine act, the first breath of life, the first mistake, the first exile, and so on. But when one begins to truly walk *the Way*, not just in belief or behavior, but in *Being*, a different truth begins to whisper through the soul.

And it is not the ego's need to understand; it is the Truth that wants to emerge.

I am not a preacher, but I have read my sacred texts, and Genesis, as told in scripture, speaks of creation from dust, a garden of peace, a serpent of temptation, and the fall of man. It paints a picture of a beginning, and yet, it leaves behind a long shadow of questions like:
Where did God come from? Who created the serpent? Why would a perfect Creator make a fragile creation? Why shame? Why fear? How come Jesus spoke of a Loving God, and that's not what I read in those books before his teachings?

These are not irreverent questions. You might have had the same. They are *the soul's nudges*, like invitations to remember something older than doctrine.

And because I love and still read gnostic texts, and because I am also drawn to teachings from other religions, my personal spiritual path has met many different beliefs along the way.

When my own remembrance began, it did not come with thunder or visions of angels. It came with inner clarity, gentle but unshakeable, a deep knowing that *the beginning we were told was not the true beginning*. Not because the story is false, but because it is incomplete.

What we call "Genesis" is not the *origin* of creation, but a *snapshot* within a vast and luminous unfolding. It is the middle of the story, like a pivotal moment when the *I AM*, having already known Itself as Light, chose to experience limitation… form… forgetting. A Divine experiment to veil Itself from Itself, and rediscover Truth through the human path.

Genesis speaks in symbols also, and I admit I don't know them all, but I know enough to believe that the garden is not just a place, it is the last echo of knowing before forgetting. The serpent is not simply evil, it is the voice of choice, of contrast. The 'fall' is not a punishment; it is a descent into experience. And the so-called exile? It was never a banishment. It was a sacred immersion into separation, into a time and place where Divine guidance seemed absent, so that reunion could one day be chosen. Willingly chosen.

When I first became aware of this, it made my heart ache with awe.
Not because I had uncovered a hidden secret, but because something inside me remembered.

I do not claim to be a scholar. I am not here to dissect ancient texts or debate timelines. Others do that. This is not a study in theology or history, it is a soul's witness. A humble offering from one who has walked deep enough into inner Truth to see that the Genesis we were taught begins long *after* the soul's first spark. And my desire was to know it from within and not just accept what I had been told.

So, I saw that there were ages before the garden, and consciousness before the serpent. There was intention, not punishment. And above all, there was, and still is... Love.

This remembrance does not erase what has been passed down. It reframes it. It frees it. It gives it the context of a much older light.

To those who have felt the questions stirring within but feared asking, know this: Your soul remembers. You are not lost. You are not doubting. You are simply awakening.

And just like when we wake up in the morning, we do not just wake up all at once, spiritual awakening is also not happening all at once.

And just like when we fall asleep at night, we do not enter deep sleep all at once. Even the dream stage comes gradually. In the same way, the spiritual dream stage, the illusion we live unfolded slowly, until we began to believe our dreams were real.

And Genesis?
It was never the first page.

It was the part where the dream deepened... for the soul could one day remember how to wake.

Afterword: Revelations in the Days that Followed

I had an incredible revelation this morning, one that finally unraveled something I have been sitting with for what feels like lifetimes.

I now understand why I could never *truly* course-correct the beliefs around poverty and abundance, no matter how many mindsets shifts I attempted, or how many times I revisited the story through inner work. And the clarity came not because I was still entangled in the ego, but because I wasn't. That's exactly *why* I could not fix it from the level where the ego controls.

Because I already came to see the ego clearly: its nature, its function, and its illusions, I was not caught in it like many others. And *that* is why I could not overcome this specific pattern anymore. I was not meant to work with it at the level of the ego at all when I was trying to shift something within a space I had already transcended. The illusion did not hold truth anymore, so there was nothing real to fix, only something deeper to understand.

And then I read something that clicked it all into place. In *The Sophia of Jesus*, a Gnostic book I have not had the chance to read before, which is not the same book as *Pistis Sophia*, the word "poverty" is used to describe the *ego experience* on Earth: "*The one who was sent to teach you and explain this to you is now with you until the end of the poverty, which the robbers have brought upon you.*"

That hit me like lightning. This *poverty* is not about being poor versus rich. It is not material lack. It is a poverty of *spirit*, a forgetting of the *I AM* richness we already are. And from there, the ego, with all its ancient data and collective subconscious data and baggage, spins the illusion that we are poor in the world, that we don't have enough, that something is missing.

But that's the key: it is not *my* root. It is the ego's root! OMG how I saw it so clearly.

And here's the wild part, every time I tried to shift from scarcity to abundance, I was still doing it on the ego's playing field, even when trying to change that in Consciousness. I was using ego logic to solve an ego-created illusion. Of course it never worked! It may work for those still operating from ego, because they can "upgrade" the belief, so to speak. But for someone who sees through it? There's nothing to shift there. I had to reach higher. I had to go to the *source* of this illusion and see it from beyond.

It's like the whole scarcity-abundance conversation is just a subtopic within the ego's playbook. I was not supposed to edit that section. Never. I was supposed to *toss out the whole chapter* and return to Truth.

Now, *"we are rich in Consciousness"* and *"abundant in I AM"* feel completely different to me. Not just a nice idea, not just a new belief, but an energetic and dimensional reality. A knowing. A homecoming. This was not a mindset shift. Because mindset shifts are done in illusion. It was a dimensional shift, one that allowed me to see that the root I was looking for was never possible to find in ego-reality.

The ego holds this ancient imprint of "poverty" and uses it as primal data, embedded in the collective unconscious, to generate the emotional, mental, and physical experience of "not enough", lack of time, love, money, energy, worth, and so on.

It hid behind its ego veil the truth that this poverty was never about being the opposite of abundance, but about being separated in Spirit. *Poverty in Spirit.*

Yet, when we are without the control of the ego, when it returns to its neutral role and rightful position, there can only be richness in Spirit. The ego simply used this poverty and richness as tools of control over the physical life experience.

It was always about the forgetfulness of Divine Identity.

*

Long before I read any of the gnostic texts I am reading today, I began saying something that came from deep within to better explain the ego's role and control: *"The ego thinks of itself as Almighty."* It felt true, not intellectually, but viscerally. It was how I explained the way ego tries to take the place of Light, impersonating the *I AM* while having no real power of its own. It was how I explained how we sometimes believed the ego to be our true identity, and why we leave it in control of our mental space. This morning, as I was reading sacred Gnostic texts, I saw words describing exactly this: a false Almighty who binds souls in forgetfulness, spreading matter through poverty of Light. By the way, poverty means a life without Light, without Spirit. I paused in awe thinking: "*Wow, how could I have known this, without ever reading it before*"? But that's the beauty of divine remembrance: what is true does not need to be taught, it rises from within. What struck me even deeper was this realization: the "Almighty" many believe to be God is not the true Source, is not the *I AM*. It is a projection of ego-consciousness, the god of the illusion. And humanity, not knowing this, has been worshipping the shadow rather than the Light. No wonder the chaos! We were deeply asleep *believing the copy was the original*. But the soul knows and remembers. It is our task to allow this remembrance. And in that remembrance, we begin to wake and see the false light for what it is, not to fear it, but to walk beyond it, toward the Real. *Oh, how I so love those revelation moments I keep having!*

*

The ego is also a belief. And that one, I did not see like this before this morning. This is why it is neutral and has no power whatsoever.
It has nothing to do with just learning to tame it or taking back control of our mental space.
The ego does not exist except in the dream state that is created from beliefs.

If everything is created in Consciousness, and *in* consciousness—in this sphere of Light where there are souls in expansion, where there is nothingness, nothing other than the beliefs of all we can experiment, be, and become... the ego is clearly also a belief.

The ego, being the neutral part, like a machine allowing us to experience physical life through the body and its five senses, is only the mechanism allowing the projection of all that we can be and become.

Knowing that we create in Consciousness and see the result in the ego-reality... and knowing that everything starts with a belief in Consciousness allowing thoughts and emotions, and therefore perception, then the ego is also a belief. I know I am repeating this, but this is how the data are recorded in our subconscious.

We believe our ego is part of ourselves.
We believe that the ego is the projector in this illusion.
We believe that our ego has control... until we stop believing it.
We made our ego to function in this dream state.

It's a belief, just like any other belief.

And just like that,
I believe I saw what I needed to know.

About the Author

Dr. Nathalie Turgeon, Ph.D., is a spiritual teacher, metaphysical practitioner, and conscious guide whose life is a living testament to the wisdom she shares. With a few decades of direct experience as a counselor, her true initiation began long before credentials or titles—rooted in a deep inner calling that shaped her path from an early age.

Her journey has not followed a straight line, but one of sacred detours, necessary forgetting, and purposeful returns to *the Way*. Like many seekers, she wandered more than once far from the Truth she now teaches—not out of failure, but to embody understanding, compassion, and mastery from within. Each step away brought her closer to the realization that she was never truly lost, only gathering what she needed to one day guide others home to themselves, without judgment.

What sets Dr. Nathalie apart is that she teaches only what she has lived. She has always wanted to "walk the talk." Her insights are not borrowed theories but hard-earned revelations—collected through her own ego-surrendering experiences, moments of grace, visions, and deep inner work. Her mission is clear: to help others free their mind, free themselves from ego illusion, awaken to their Higher Self, and live from pure Love.

In her 50s, she went back to school, following an inner call to expand her studies. She holds a Ph.D. in Philosophy with a specialization in Metaphysical Counseling. She made it her mission to explore, for her dissertation, the topic of gratitude: *Gratitude as a Spiritual Mind Treatment for Mental Health*, following her master's thesis on *Reaching the Summit of Consciousness Through Meditation Like Great Masters and Prophets Did*.

While she self-published workbooks on gratitude, Ho'oponopono, and faith, it is only recently that she stepped fully into her lifelong dream of allowing her inner author to share knowingness in book format—speaking not just to the mind, but awakening something beyond the ego veils, allowing the soul to shine through. Whether writing, teaching, or simply being, Dr. Nathalie transmits spiritual truth as one who *is* it.

Her core message and her mantra?

"Breathe in, let go of all your ego-based thoughts and vision, see from your Soul… and Love Out."

nathalieturgeon.com

breatheinloveoutcenter.com

www.ingramcontent.com/pod-product-compliance
Lightning Source LLC
Chambersburg PA
CBHW061730070526
44583CB00024B/3083